JUPITER

PLANETS IN OUR SOLAR SYSTEM

CHILDREN'S ASTRONOMY EDITION

SPEEDY
PUBLISHING

Speedy Publishing LLC
40 E. Main St. #1156
Newark, DE 19711
www.speedypublishing.com

Jupiter is the fifth
planet from the Sun.

Jupiter is
the largest
in the Solar
System, more
than 1300
Earths could
fit inside it.

Jupiter is the fastest spinning planet in the Solar System.

Jupiter is a
gas giant with
a mass more
than 300 times
the mass of
the Earth.

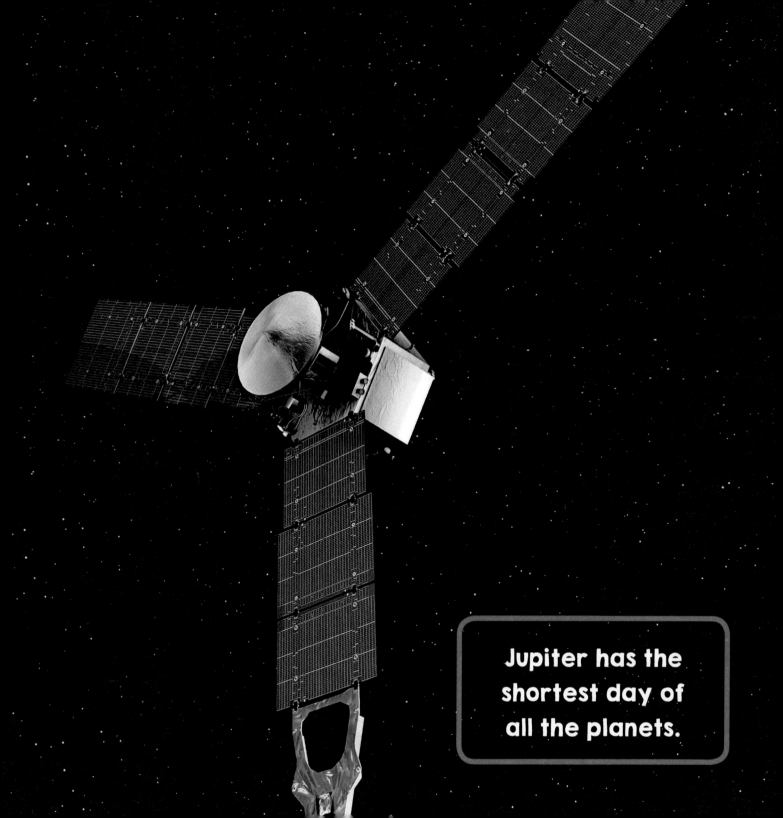

Jupiter has the
shortest day of
all the planets.

Jupiter has
a diameter
of 142,750
kilometres.

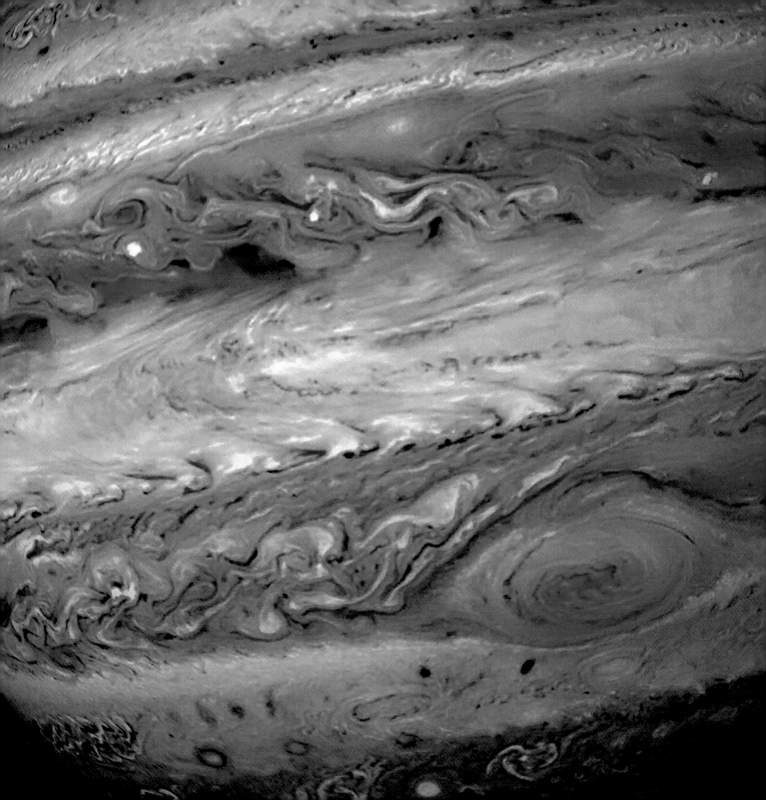

Jupiter has three
very faint rings.

Jupiter is about
777 million
kilometres
away from
the Sun.

Jupiter orbits the Sun once every 11.8 Earth years.

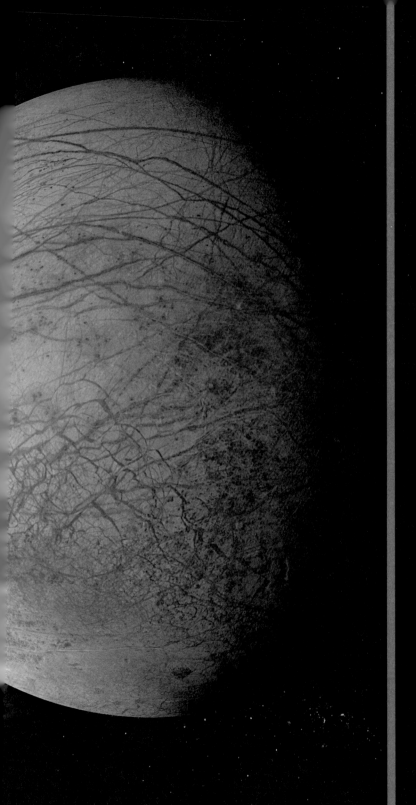

Jupiter is primarily composed of hydrogen with a quarter of its mass being helium.

Jupiter's name came
from the Roman
god of mythology.

Jupiter has at least 67 moons, including the four large Galilean moons discovered by Galileo Galilei in 1610.

Jupiter's moon
Ganymede is the
largest moon in
the solar system.

Jupiter has many storms raging on the surface, the great red spot is a huge storm that has been raging for over three hundred years.

Winds inside the great red spot storm reach speeds of about 270 mph.

Jupiter is the 4th brightest object in the sky and was known to astronomers of ancient times.

Jupiter has an extremely strong magnetic field, you would weigh two and a half times as much as you would on Earth.

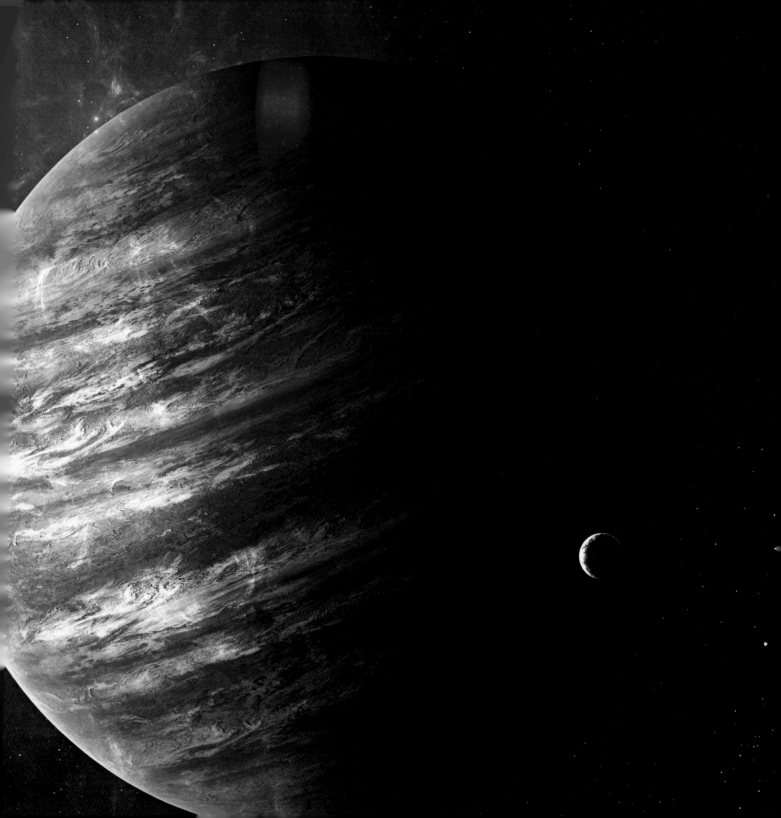

Thick, colorful
clouds of
deadly
poisonous
gases
surround
Jupiter.

Jupiter has the largest planetary atmosphere in the Solar System.

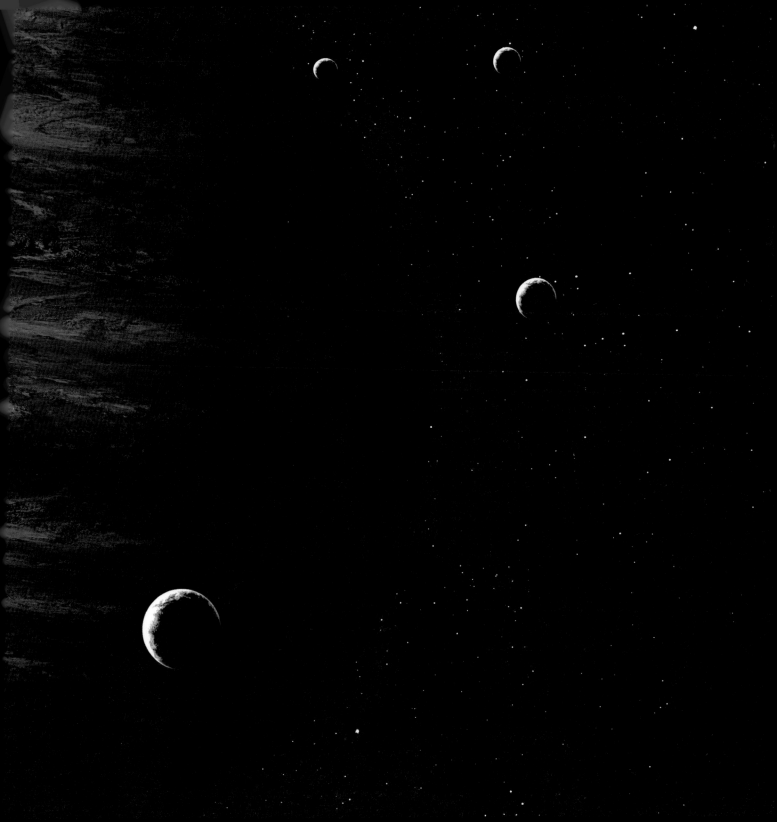

Made in United States
North Haven, CT
14 March 2023

34060504R00024